Nature's Children

WOODPECKERS

Tim Harris

GROLIER
EDUCATIONAL

FACTS IN BRIEF

Classification of Woodpeckers

Class: *Aves* (birds)
Order: *Piciformes* (woodpeckers, toucans, and others)
Family: *Picidae* (woodpecker family)
Genus: There are 23 genera of true woodpeckers.
Species: There are 182 species of true woodpeckers.

World distribution.   Worldwide except remote islands, Antarctica, Australasia, and the Sahara, Arabian, and Gobi deserts.

Habitat.   Mostly forests and woods. Other species found in savanna, farmland towns, and above the tree line on mountains.

Distinctive physical characteristics.   Size and color variable. All have strong beaks and short legs.

Habits.   Active in daytime. Most species spend much of their time feeding on tree trunks and branches. Others hop on the ground. Flight is very undulating (bounding).

Diet.   Mainly insects, especially ants; also other bugs, fruit, berries, nuts, sap, and other birds' eggs and young.

© 2001 Brown Partworks Limited
Printed and bound in U.S.A.
Edited by Jens Thomas

Published by:

GROLIER
EDUCATIONAL

Sherman Turnpike, Danbury, Connecticut 06816

Library of Congress Cataloging-in-Publication Data

Woodpeckers.
     p. cm. -- (Nature's children. Set 7)
   ISBN 0-7172-5552-2 (alk. paper) -- ISBN 0-7172-5531-X (set)
   1. Woodpeckers--Juvenile literature. [1. Woodpeckers.] I. Grolier Educational (Firm)
II. Series.

QL696.P56 W66 2001
598.7'2--dc21

00-067242

Contents

Which is the most famous woodpecker in the world? No question about it, the title belongs to the cartoon character Woody Woodpecker, whose laughing call and wood-shattering beak is known in every corner of the world. In fact, real-life woodpeckers have every bit as much character. The problem is, not too many people get to see their antics because woodpeckers spend most of their time hidden away in woods and forests.

Woodpeckers are colorful, skillful, and very clever birds. They are expert climbers and woodworkers, and some of them do things that are unique in the world of birds. Some visit backyards in towns, others can fly thousands of miles, and a few live on the tops of mountains. Read on to find out more about these amazing birds.

Opposite page:
A male yellow-bellied sapsucker brings a wasp back to his nest.

5

Meet the Family

Opposite page:
A green woodpecker outside its tree-trunk home.

Animals that are similar but not quite the same are grouped into families. Scientists do this to help us understand the relationships among the different types. If someone tells us they have an automobile, they don't have to describe every detail of it for us to picture what it looks like. We can be pretty sure it has a steering wheel, an engine, and four wheels.

It is similar with birds and other animals. The world's 182 types of true woodpeckers are alike in lots of ways: they have a strong beak, short legs, and stiff tail feathers. Most live in woods and forests. That is not to say that woodpeckers are all look-alikes. Far from it. They come in all sizes and colors, and they live in all kinds of different places. Woodpeckers are not the only birds that climb trees: nuthatches, treecreepers, woodcreepers, wrynecks, and piculets also spend much of their lives on tree trunks and branches.

The Woodpecker Kingdom

Wherever you live, you can be pretty sure that you're not far from a woodpecker. They are found in most parts of the world, though not in Australia, New Zealand, New Guinea, or the frozen continent of Antarctica. Woodpeckers also avoid the world's driest places, such as the Sahara, Arabian, and Gobi deserts. Different animals and birds prefer different types of place. These places are called habitats.

Some woodpeckers can get by in a range of different conditions; others are very choosy and are only found where certain types of tree grow. Most woodpeckers live in forests, but others are quite happy in countryside with only scattered trees. Some make their homes in gardens and visit backyard feeders. A few live where there are no trees at all, digging for their food in cacti or in the ground.

Opposite page:
This gila woodpecker has made its home in a saguaro cactus. Gila woodpeckers live in the southwestern United States and northwestern Mexico.

Up, Up, and Away

Woodpeckers are smart birds. Like other birds, they can fly and hop, and with their powerful beaks they can dig holes in the wood of trees. Their most impressive skill is their ability to climb trees, something they make look easy.

We climb because it is fun, but it does not really matter whether we can do it or not. For woodpeckers climbing is very important. Woodpeckers feed on insects and spiders under the bark of trees. If they could not climb, they would not be able to get at this food.

What makes woodpeckers so good at climbing? Their toes are specially adapted for grasping vertical tree trunks, with two toes facing forward and two backward. Their legs are strong, and their tail feathers are stiffer than those of other birds are. This makes a difference because it means a woodpecker can use its tail as a support when it climbs a tree.

Acrobatics

The smallest woodpeckers can perform acrobatics better than anything you will ever see at the circus. They look like they can defy gravity as they run upside down along the undersides of branches and hang upside down underneath food. It is not a game for them, though—they do it so they can get at the food they need to stay alive.

The very best acrobatic performers are the piculets. They are tiny relations of the true woodpeckers that are as happy living in small bushes as they are in trees.

The giants of the woodpecker family cannot perform the same tricks, but there are few more impressive sights in the natural world than watching one of them making its way up the vertical trunk of a large tree faster than any human can. They do it in a series of jumps.

Opposite page: A red-crowned woodpecker makes hanging upside down look easy!

A Shape for Life

All woodpeckers have a sturdy beak, and they need it! It is the tool they use to get at their food. They use it in several different ways: to pull bark off tree branches; to chisel into wood for insects; to dig holes in wood to create nest cavities; to grab hold of their food; and to dig into the ground in search of ants.

To chisel into a tree, the wood has to be struck very hard. A woodpecker's beak has been measured hitting the bark of a tree at 15 miles per hour (25 kilometers per hour), and many hammer blows are needed to dig a hole into the wood.

So why don't woodpeckers get headaches? One reason is that strong muscles at the base of the beak act like the shock absorbers in an automobile, soaking up the pressure of the powerful hammering.

Birds of a Feather

Some birds are rather dull to look at. Not so woodpeckers, which are some of the most colorful birds in the world. Most show brightly colored feathers, and many have vivid patterns. Some are spotted, some are striped, some have zigzags, and some even have heart-shaped patterns on their wings. Woodpeckers come in yellow, green, brown, pink, red, black, and white. Some have all these colors on them.

Most woodpeckers have a patch of bright red or yellow somewhere on their head. This splash of color is often referred to as a "badge." Its size and shape often show whether the bird is a male or a female, or whether it is an adult or a young bird. It is important for woodpeckers to help them know who they are dealing with as they go about their business. It also helps humans understand more about the way that woodpeckers behave.

Opposite page: *Its brightly colored red badge means this gila woodpecker is easy to recognize.*

On the Menu

What's your favorite food? If woodpeckers were able to answer this question, they would not be able to agree on an answer, but ants would get more votes than anything else. Most types of woodpecker eat lots of other insects, especially wood-boring beetles, and spiders.

Their very varied diet also includes fruit, berries, and acorns. Some species (types) have a sweet tooth and can't resist the sap in trees. A few break into the nests of other birds to eat their eggs or babies. Some are prepared to try out more unusual food: scorpions, lizards, and even shellfish. Of course, woodpeckers get thirsty as well as hungry. They get their water mainly from small puddles that sometimes form in the forks of trees.

A female green woodpecker looking for ants in the grass.

Secret Weapons

Imagine what it would be like trying to catch tiny insects that live deep inside the trunk of a tree. Sometimes these insect burrows are so narrow that you would need a pin to get them out. Woodpeckers don't have pins, but they need to get at the insects all the same because they are an important part of the bird's diet. So how do they do it?

Woodpeckers get around this problem by using an amazing secret weapon. Their secret is a tongue that can be stuck out far beyond the end of the beak to get into even the narrowest crack and hole. That's not all. The tongue is very sticky, and it has tiny spikes near the tip. So once the tongue has shot out and touched the bug, there is little chance of it getting away. The woodpecker quickly reels its tongue in like a fishing line and swallows the juicy morsel it has caught.

Opposite page:
This lineated woodpecker can use its long tongue to reach bugs hidden deep inside the tree.

21

Pecking and Tapping

Opposite page: *Woodpeckers can cause a lot of damage to trees.*

Woody Woodpecker in the cartoons can drill his way through just about anything. Real-life woodpeckers are pretty amazing, too. But they are clever enough to know that a soft, rotten tree is easier to get into than a hard one. So, first a hungry woodpecker will test out the tree with a few gentle taps to see if it is going to be hard work. If it is very rotten, a few tugs at the bark may be enough to reveal the insects and spiders below.

If not, full-scale demolition work will be required: the woodpecker will draw its head back and hammer at the tree with very powerful blows. If the bird sees a crack, it may widen it by sticking its beak in and twisting, or it may use its tongue to feel for insects.

Break It Up

Some of the food we eat is too large to swallow in one bite, so we use a knife, fork, or spoon to cut it into bite-sized chunks. Woodpeckers too have the same problem, but they can't use cutlery. They do not let this stop them, however.

Woodpeckers have found clever ways of smashing up their food. They will take a cherrystone, large beetle, or pine cone and wedge it into the gap between two branches of a tree, known as an anvil. With the food fixed securely, the woodpecker can attack it with its beak until it breaks into pieces that are small enough to be eaten.

If an anvil works well, the woodpecker will use it again and again: up to 5,000 pine cones have been found underneath a very good one. Some anvils may even be used by more than one woodpecker.

Opposite page: *The pine cones scattered at the base of this tree stump show that this must be a very popular anvil.*

Incredible Hoarders

Opposite page:
*An acorn
woodpecker
arriving at a
granary.*

After we have been shopping, we don't eat all the food at once. Some of it goes in the freezer to be eaten later. That's what some woodpeckers do too. When food is plentiful, they store it for another time when there may not be as much of it around.

Instead of a freezer, acorn woodpeckers build "granaries" to store their favorite food of acorns. They dig out holes in the trunk of a tree and hammer an acorn into each one for safe keeping. The granaries are looked after carefully by the woodpeckers. Some granaries are very old and may contain as many as 50,000 holes. The acorns are hammered into the holes securely, so it is difficult for an intruder to pry them out. If a thief does appear, a group of acorn woodpeckers will chase it away. They are truly the top hoarders of the world of birds!

Sweet Supply

Some woodpeckers have a most unusual diet. They drill neat rings or spirals of holes around the trunks of trees to get at the tree's sweet and energy-rich sap. Woodpeckers called sapsuckers do this the best. When the sap leaks from the holes, they lick it up. This sweet supply is not abandoned after one visit; as long as the sap remains, it will be visited again and again whenever the woodpecker gets hungry.

Some other animals are very grateful to these sapsucking woodpeckers. Other birds, squirrels, and mice feed at the sap wells after the woodpecker has left. Sapsuckers feed on sap year-round, though they can eat other kinds of food as well. The breeding season is the time when sapsuckers are most likely to eat other kinds of food.

Opposite page: *This young yellow-bellied sapsucker has cut several holes into the tree to get at the sweet sap inside.*

All Friends Together

In colder parts of the world food may be harder to get in the wintertime, and birds may forget about their territorial battles and join forces to search for it. Many of the smaller woodpeckers join up with flocks of other birds like chickadees at this time of year.

This has two advantages. First, with more pairs of eyes there is a greater chance of food being found. Second, with more birds on the lookout for danger there is less chance of a predator (a bird or animal that eats others) making a surprise attack. If woodpeckers can get by this way, it saves them the trouble of flying to warmer regions for the winter.

This is not the only time woodpeckers will gang up together. Acorn woodpeckers live in groups of up to 15 birds; and if another bird tries to get at the acorns in their larder, they will unite to chase off the intruder.

This male chestnut woodpecker is sharing a meal with blue-gray and palm tanagers.

Homebodies

Most woodpeckers aren't great travelers. They are quite content to stick around in the same area of woodland or countryside throughout the year. After all, why do they need to move when they can get what they need at home?

Not all woodpeckers have life this easy, though. Some live where it is so cold in winter that they cannot find enough food to stay alive. If they stayed, they could starve, so instead they take a long winter vacation and head south. Some of the woodpeckers that breed in northern Canada fly south (migrate) each fall to southern parts of the United States. This is a distance of more than 1,000 miles.

A few sometimes get swept far out to sea in storms and either die in the Atlantic Ocean or get to hitch a ride on ships going to Europe. A sapsucker was once seen tapping on the mast of an ocean liner bound for the UK, many miles out to sea!

Opposite page: *A green woodpecker can find life very hard in the winter.*

Woodpeckers and People

Opposite page:
This great spotted woodpecker is enjoying a meal from the feeder in a backyard.

People and woodpeckers get on pretty well in most places. Woodpeckers' acrobatic antics at backyard bird feeders certainly help make people like them. It is not always like this, however. In parts of the world woodpeckers eat fruit and nuts that are grown to sell in stores. Elsewhere, they have been known to hammer holes into wooden houses. In Israel they have drilled into the irrigation pipes carrying water to farms, making the pipes leak.

More serious than the problems that woodpeckers make for people are those that we create for them. Each time a forest is cut down, hundreds of woodpeckers are left homeless. This is a very big problem in many places. Woodpeckers that need large territories suffer especially badly. Two of the world's biggest woodpeckers, the imperial woodpecker and the ivory-billed woodpecker, are now thought to be extinct because of people destroying the woods where they live.

Attracting Attention

Like other birds, woodpeckers pair up to have young. This partnership lasts only for one breeding season, but during this time the two partners are loyal to each other. Before attracting a mate, the male woodpecker sets up a territory. It is an area in which other males of the same species are not allowed. The reason for this is to make sure that they have enough food to provide for their young family. It would be no good for the mom to lay eggs if the parents couldn't provide for the youngsters once they had hatched.

The dad-to-be calls loudly and drums near the nest hole that he has hammered out. All this racket serves two purposes: It warns other males to stay away, and it is an invitation to any females in the area to "Come and see the beautiful home I've made."

Showing Off

Once a female has been attracted by the sound of a male's drumming, he will show off to impress her. If she is impressed by him, she may join in. Sometimes both birds will drum on a tree together. Some woodpeckers look at each other and sway their heads from side to side or point their beaks skyward. Others chase each other around and around the trees or show off by flying around with their wings flapping slowly, a bit like big butterflies.

The males and females of some species feed each other just to prove how much they care for each other. These actions all help draw the two birds more closely together. This is very important because they'll have to depend on each other during the busy period ahead when they are bringing up their babies.

Home Sweet Home

Many birds lay their eggs in flimsy nests of twigs and moss built in the branches of trees. Not woodpeckers, though. Their ability to dig holes in wood gives them a special advantage: by laying their eggs inside a tree, they are protected from the weather and from animals or other birds that might want to eat them.

Digging out holes can be hard work, though; it may take two weeks from start to finish. So if a woodpecker can find a hole excavated (dug out) by another bird, and if it can kick that bird out, then it can get a new home with the least effort. And that is what happens sometimes.

What about woodpeckers that live in areas where there are no trees? They have to dig elsewhere. Andean flickers, which live high in the Andes Mountains, burrow their holes into the ground. And gilded flickers, which inhabit the dry deserts of California, chisel out their homes in giant cacti.

Inside the Egg

Female woodpeckers usually lay one batch, or clutch, of white eggs every year. Sometimes the female may have the time and energy to lay two clutches. The batch of eggs may contain as few as three eggs or as many as 12. Experiments have shown that if an egg is taken away from the mother, she will lay another egg to replace it.

The baby birds develop inside the hard shells of the eggs. While the clutch of eggs is in the nest, the eggs have to be incubated (kept warm). If they were left for more than a few minutes, the developing babies inside would die. Mom and dad take turns sitting on the eggs and keeping them warm.

Baby woodpeckers are ready to hatch from their eggs more quickly than most birds. After about two weeks they peck holes in the egg shells with the help of a bony knob on their beak, called an egg tooth, and break out. Welcome to the big wide world!

Opposite page:
A baby northern flicker being fed by one of his parents.

Help at Hand

It's tough work being a woodpecker parent.
While mom and dad take turns sitting on the
eggs, their partner has to go in search of food.
This goes on for two weeks until the babies
hatch, then life gets even busier since there are
even more mouths to be fed.

Some woodpeckers have life a little easier:
they have helpers while they are sitting. These
helpers are woodpeckers of the same species
that don't have their own eggs or chicks to
look after. They come in to take a turn at
sitting on the eggs, giving the parents a
welcome break. Most helpers are thought to be
male birds, and sometimes the oldest of them
will take over the territory if the breeding male
happens to disappear.

It is hard work being a woodpecker parent, bringing food to the nest and carrying rubbish away.

Feeding Time

Baby woodpeckers cannot fend for themselves. They are born blind and don't have any feathers, though they grow quickly. Both parents feed them. Like baby humans, they are fed on mushed-up food first before they are old enough to be given solids. The speed at which they grow up is amazing, and unlike baby humans, they can start to fend for themselves within a few weeks.

After about a month they are able to leave the nest, though many woodpecker parents continue to feed them for some time afterward. Sometimes mom and dad share the responsibility for helping the young through their first days out of the nest. Sometimes only one parent helps. With no experience of the outside world the young ones are constantly in danger from bigger animals or birds that may see them as a tasty snack.

Words to Know

Adapted A feature of an animal that has changed over time to make it better suited to a particular habitat or way of life.

Anvil The gap between two branches of a tree, which a woodpecker uses to break up food into bite-sized chunks.

Badge The brightly colored patch on a woodpecker's head.

Drumming The noise a woodpecker makes by knocking its beak against a tree in order to attract a mate.

Egg tooth A toothlike point on a chick's beak used to help it crack its way out of the egg.

Extinct When all of the animals of a particular species have died, and there are no more left anywhere in the world.

Family Animals that are similar but not quite the same are said to be of the same "family."

Habitat The area in which an animal naturally lives.

Incubate To keep eggs warm so that they will hatch.

Mate To come together to produce young.

Migrate To make a long seasonal journey, usually in search of food or to reach breeding areas.

Predator An animal that hunts other animals for food.

Territory Area where an animal hunts or breeds. The animal defends its territory against other animals.

INDEX

Cover Photo: Bill Coster / NHPA
Photo Credits: Robert Erwin / NHPA, page 4; Roger Wilmshurst, pages 7, 19, 35, 41;
Daniel Heuclin / NHPA, page 8; Neil Bowman, pages 11, 12, 28, 31; Bill Coster / NHPA,
page 15; Roland Seitre / Still Pictures, page 16; Kevin Schafer / NHPA, page 20; Stephen
Krasemann / NHPA, pages 23, 42; Dr Eckhart Pott / NHPA, page 24; Kevin Schafer / Still
Pictures, page 27; Paal Hermansen / NHPA, page 32; Norbert Wu / Still Pictures, pages
38–39; Stephen Dalton / NHPA, page 45.